To Lee and Gail McTaggart

It's a cerebral game,

so remember, less is more.

Best wishes

Tom Trebelhorn

Christmas 2000

GOLF MADE DIFFICULT

▼▼▼

Tom Trowbridge

illustrations by Bob Schulenberg

THREE BRIDGES PRESS
NEW YORK

Book design by Jane Ethe

ISBN 0-9679183-0-8
Library of Congress Control Number: 00-090694

To Ken Frank

ACKNOWLEDGMENTS

▼▼▼

With appreciation for their friendship:

David Beck, Bob Burch, Ray Calamaro, Barclay Collins, Tony Corso, John Huggins, Mike Mewshaw, Peter Pettus and Don Welsh.

Two friends — John Schremp and his co-conspirator, Dale Dodrill — deserve special mention. I am indebted to John, literally, for regularly introducing me to new ways to lose money on the golf course. Dale, in turn, showed me how, by playing automatic presses along with "greenies," "sandies," "barkies," "gurgles" and other trash, a $2 Nassau can put a college fund in jeopardy.

I also thank my wife Nancy and our children, Thomas, Carrie and Annie. All of them supported this project, some by offering substantive comments, others by discreetly looking the other way.

TABLE OF CONTENTS

▼▼▼

INTRODUCTION

▼▼▼

Each Monday morning it's always the same.
The golfers all gather to talk of their game.

The language they use, it's rather bizarre.
You hear "bogie," "birdie" and of something called "par."

They talk of "hosels" and "cross-handed" grips,
Of "dormie" and "stymie," "Mulligans" and the "yips."

They play "Calcuttas," some "rounds" are disasters.
The "Honda" and the "Hope" mean less than the "Masters."

There's the "waggle," "gimmie" and "hitting stiff to pins."
Some people lose "sides," while others win "skins."

▼▼▼

One prefers "balata," but is down on "soft spikes."
Someone else bought a new "grooveless face" he quite likes.

There are square and V grooves, there are "leading edges."
They talk of how much "bounce" they like in their wedges.

They compare "greens fees" at the places they went,
And discuss their grasses — Bermuda or bent.

Each course has a "slope" and greens, a "Stimpmeter rating."
They talk new equipment — like shafts with chrome plating.

They'd all like to have the newest of the new
Like a driver with a "tungsten gravity screw."

Some shots they try to "crush," others they want to "sink."
There are "links," but you learn, no such thing as a "link."

Everyone of them wants to increase clubhead speed.
They debate who was best, Nicklaus, Hogan or Snead.

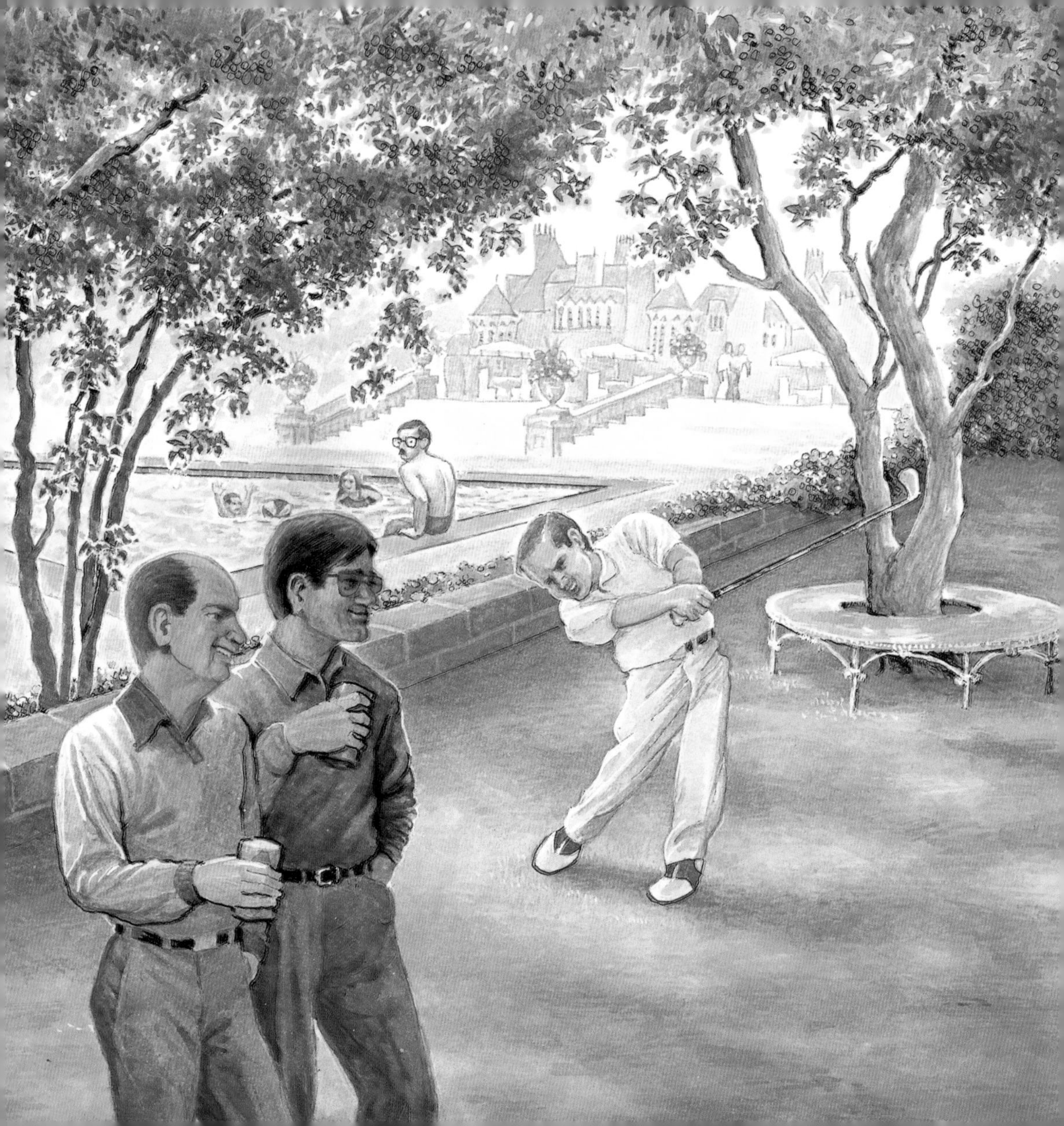

▼▼▼

There's talk of Penick and the secrets he'd teach.
They'd love to play "Winged Foot," "Muirfield" and "Pebble Beach."

Sometimes they play "medal," sometimes they play "match."
Most have "handicaps," but the boss is "scratch."

There are "slices" and "draws" and "shanks" and "duck hooks."
You try to talk tennis and get funny looks.

They call it exercise, but that's only talk.
At most courses they play, they're not allowed to walk.

At the company outing you feel like a fool.
They play golf with the boss; you wade in the pool.

Your career is on hold, and there it could stay.
Without golf you are stuck; you must learn how to play.

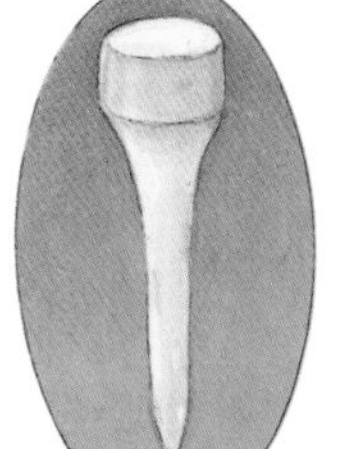

THE EQUIPMENT
THE CHOICES

▼▼▼

Before you learn the swing, etiquette or the rules,
You must equip yourself with a set of golf's tools.

Fourteen clubs or "sticks" are what you'll have to get,
Woods, irons and a putter to make up your set.

Something you won't know (there's no reason you should),
Most "woods" come in metal, they're not made of wood.

They come in steel, alloys and aluminum — milled.
Some are graphite-faced or with core that's foam filled.

For a wood that's quite light, you might want to try
The latest metal, titanium ("ti").

And the wood right now that's most highly prized,
Has a hollow ti head that is called "megasized."

There are the purists, though, both men and women,
Who like woods that are carved from blocks of persimmon.

▼▼▼

Start with the driver, to be used from the tees.
You must first pick the loft, (it's measured in degrees).

From eight to thirteen the degrees are found,
To make balls go high, or stay close to the ground.

Selecting a shaft is what should come next.
How stiff do you want it when you swing and it's flexed?

When that's done you should pick the right weight and feel.
There's graphite (with boron), also chrome-plated steel.

You might like a shaft with titanium sleeve
That's filament wound or with carbon weave.

To hit the drive straight and away from trouble
They've come up with a shaft that's shaped like a bubble.

You'll want grip that won't slip in hot or wet weather.
They're made out of rubber (they used to be leather).

When you've found a driver that feels good in your hands,
Add a three then five wood — there are dozens of brands.

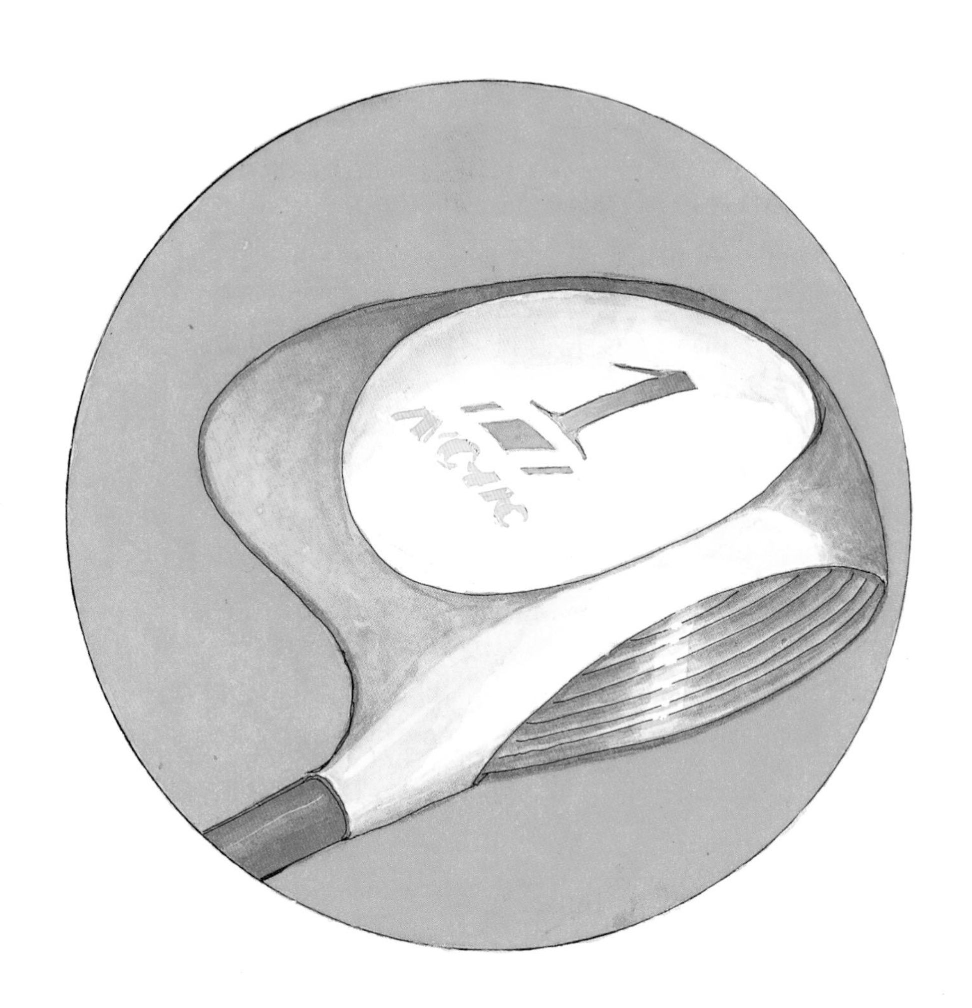

▼ ▼ ▼

As for irons — the best? That's long been debated —
Investment cast, forged, or perimeter weighted?

(Forged is mainly for pros who play for a living.
Perimeter weighting is much more forgiving.)

Irons come in sets, two's as low as you should go.
(A one iron's quite macho, carried mainly for show.)

Next come the wedges — they have the most loft —
For going high (not far) and landing real soft.

Two or three wedges? Preferences keep switching.
One's for sand, one's for lobs, another's for pitching.

There's a putter, you'll find, to suit every palate.
The heads are round or square, the blade and the mallet.

There's gooseneck, there's offset, but some think what's best
Is an extra-long one you hold close to your chest.

THE PURCHASE

▼▼▼

At a store like a warehouse this equipment's displayed.
They have scores of brands, every model and grade.

To a salesman you say that you've heard it said
All you need is something with a shaft and a head.

Looking pained he asks: "Would it not be a shame
If your clubs limited the level of your game?"

"Think of golf as war, and when you attack,
You don't want your weapons to be holding you back."

"If you're smart," he says, "you'll take my advice.
In selecting your clubs, forget about price."

"Take these irons," he points, "they're the latest version.
Tests have shown that they have great shot dispersion."

"Most of the weight is placed in the toe and the heel.
For cavity backs these babies have great feel."

"They give the ball a nice angle of ascent,
And cut down on misshits by thirty percent."

UM COPPER
BRONZ
CAVITY INSET

BLADE
GOOSENECK
PUTTERS
BULLSEYE
MALLET

▼▼▼

"Let's talk offset," he adds. "It's often excessive.
Note that with these clubs, the offset's progressive."

You nod at "offset," adding: "That dispersion sounds good."
Trying hard to sound as though you've understood.

"For your driver," he says, "go with twelve degrees.
And get a big head, like 300 cc's."

This information, all it does is confuse.
Then you think that club names might be a way to choose.

There are drivers with names like "The Launcher" or "Wailer,"
"The Blaster," "Enforcer," "Screamer" or "Air Mailer."

You're torn between two — the "Crusher" and "Whopper" —
And irons in steel or beryllium copper.

It's hopeless deciding which way you should go,
So you resort to eenie, meenie, miney and mo.

You spend all the money your wife said you could bring.
Equipped, now you're ready to tackle The Swing.

THE SWING

▼▼▼

You drive to a range, put a ball on a tee,
And mimic some pros you've seen on TV.

The result, when you swing, is not what you expect.
You hear "whoosh" not "click." You have failed to connect.

This should be easy, right? You'll soon be improving.
It can't be hard to hit a ball that's not moving.

An adjustment, no doubt, maybe one move to change.
You seek out "Joe the Pro," the guy who owns the range.

"Something's wrong," you say, "with the swing that I make.
I'd like it fixed soon. How long should that take?"

"The golf swing," he says, "is rather like a song.
If one part is off, then the whole thing is wrong."

"Who has mastered the swing? Their numbers are few.
Many play golf for years, but still haven't a clue."

"And if you don't start young, it's so much tougher
Not to play the game like a hacker or duffer."

"You're no spring chicken, and that's a concern
But I think you'll do fine. Just listen and learn."

DON'T LOOK UP!
FOLLOW THROUGH...
TAKE DEAD AIM —
TEMPO...
SWING, DON'T HIT...
Keep head steady...
Straight left arm...
RELAX.
FULL PIVOT
TUCK RIGHT ELBOW IN
... Pick up dry cleaning...
SLOW BACKSWING
TURN, don't sway -
full pivot...
clear left hip...
cock wrists at top...
BIG SHOULDER TURN...
TEMPO!
WATCH the BALL -

THE LESSON

GRIP, STANCE AND ADDRESS

▼▼▼

First grab hold of the club. For the pressure that's right
Think of holding a bird, not too loose or too tight.

For the grip, place your hands like you're going to clap.
To join them pick a grip — interlock or overlap.

Turn your hands to the point where they feel they belong.
Some like a "weak" grip, others prefer "strong."

Now turn to the stance, find the one that works best
When, with club in your hands, the ball is "addressed."

Where you put your feet affects the path of the blade.
A closed stance for a "draw," open for a "fade."

With a stance that is square, the ball won't curve either way.
It will go straight ahead (at least that's what they say).

With feet spread apart, and weight evenly based,
Bend a bit at the knees, lean forward at the waist.

Your back should be straight (if that's how you're built).
So don't slouch or hunch when your back's in a tilt.

Position the head so it's right on a line
That runs straight through the neck and joins up with the spine.

The head of the club will be in the right place
When the ball and target line up with the club face.

THE BACKSWING

▼▼▼

Check your stance, grip and arms, each part of the address,
Then begin the backswing with a slight "forward press."

The club's takeaway, it should be one piece,
With a slow and smooth speed that doesn't increase.

With the club going back your weight should be shifted.
The shoulders keep turning, they shouldn't be lifted.

The right leg should take nearly all of your weight.
The left arm, while not stiff, should be almost straight.

As the club goes back, what plane should it keep?
Some say it should be flat. Many, though, prefer steep.

When the club nears the top, you should be trying
To tuck the right elbow in, so it isn't "flying."

At the top of the swing, the wrists should be cocked,
The right knee slightly bent, but it shouldn't be locked.

There's one school that says you should pause at the top.
Another says keep moving, it's a mistake to stop.

Whether to pause or not, that's your election.
What's key is a smooth change of direction.

THE DOWNSWING

▼▼▼

Now comes the downswing, your body is ready.
Though your limbs have all moved, your head must stay steady.

When you swing the club down, don't start with the hands.
If you "hit from the top," you won't like where the ball lands.

To start the club down, some say the move that's ideal
Is a subtle one — just plant the left heel.

There are many, though, who will disagree.
What you must do, they say, is to slide the left knee.

Still others will say avoid a shoulder dip.
Pause for a second, then uncoil the left hip.

There are teachers who say that won't work (or it might).
Uncoil a hip, true, not the left but the right.

"Push right hip," "pull the left," both tips Joe's rejected.
"On most golfers," he says, "both hips are connected."

To get the most speed from the swing that you've made,
Try to keep your wrists cocked, so the hit is "delayed."

The club's all the way down, it's dropped into the "slot."
The ball's left the club face; you think you're done. *You're* not.

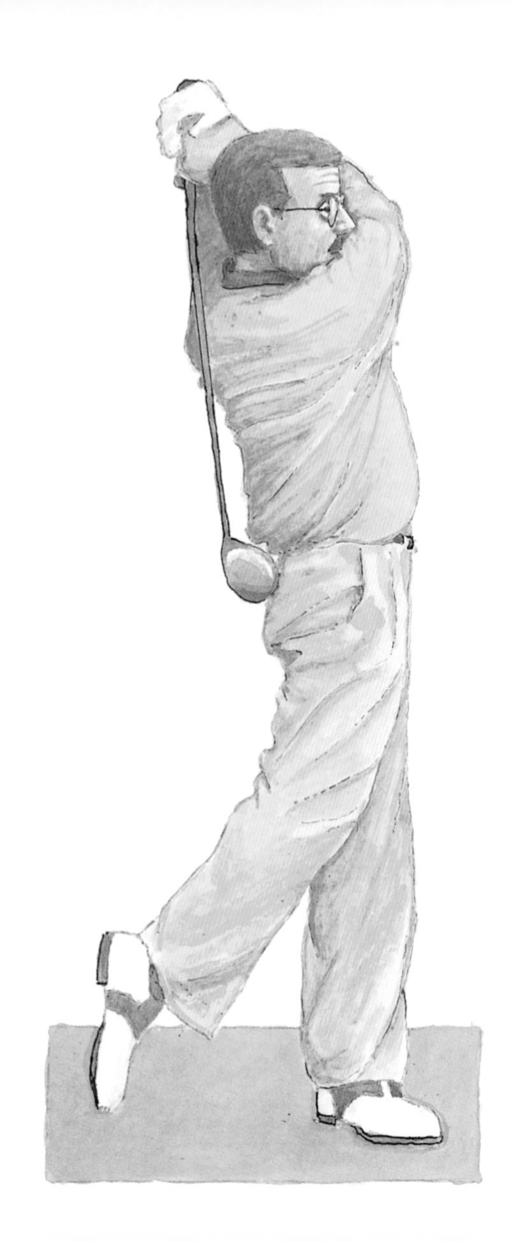

THE FOLLOWTHROUGH

▼▼▼

What your body does now affects where the ball goes.
Though it's quite far away, somehow the ball knows.

It knows, for example, if your hands have led.
It certainly knows if you've lifted your head.

All your weight now must move from where it's been put,
Back the other way and onto the left foot.

The swing continues against a "firm left side,"
While the club face has gone from in to outside.

The finish should be smooth and under control.
Your body should be turned and facing the hole.

Is your finish complete? There's a good way to check.
The shaft should be laying on the back of your neck.

You're steady, you're balanced, your followthrough feels good.
Now the ball that's been hit will go where it should.

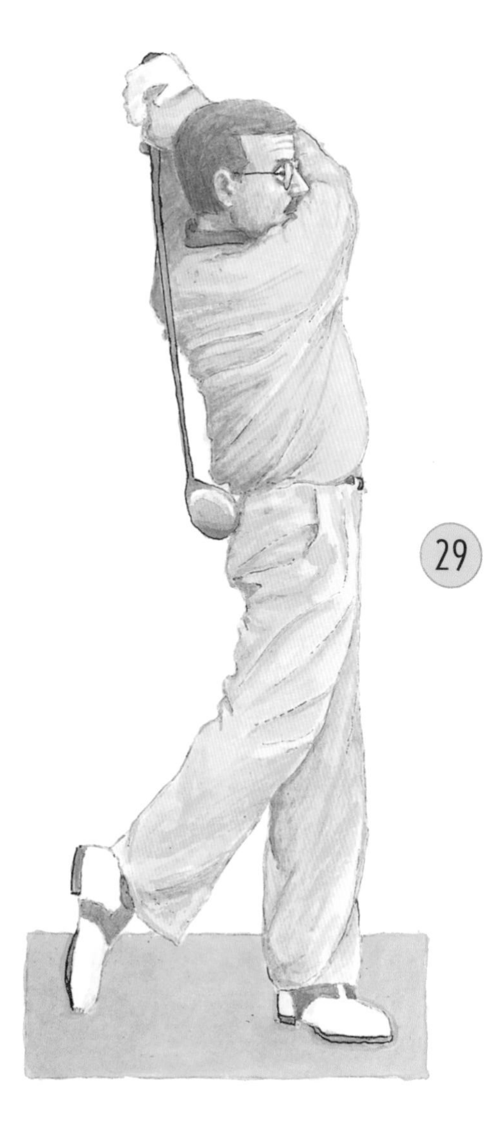

PRACTICE — GRIM REALITY

▼▼▼

You've had lessons, watched tapes, and so you won't forget,
You've hit balls at the range and into a net.

You practice 'til you ache, and your hands become raw.
You're determined to fix the slightest swing flaw.

But when part of your swing has been corrected,
Something else, you find, has been neglected.

As you try to make sure your left arm isn't bent,
You look up too soon to see where the ball went.

While you concentrate hard on a smooth takeaway,
You forget to turn and do more of a sway.

Your alignment is good (that's where the club's faced),
But you stand much too tall, and don't bend at the waist.

When you start to worry about what the ball will do,
You stop your swing too soon, and don't follow through.

Then you read that to help the swing's execution,
Many find that swing aids can be a solution.

You're desperate now, you don't care what their prices,
And so you stock up on a bunch of devices.

You get a gadget to check if your tempo is smooth,
And a gizmo to see that your head doesn't move.

▼▼▼

To make sure when they cock that your hands don't twist,
You get a strap for your arms and a brace for a wrist.

To get a good stroke for when you're on the green,
You furnish your den with a putting machine.

Then someone tells you the best advice you'll find
Is forget all you've learned — clear it from your mind.

RULES OF GOLF
Vol. 46
HOW to PLAY GOLF
PLAY GOLF!
GOLF AND YOU!
golf
GOLF

THE RULES

▼▼▼

In this game you try for the least, not the most,
In the number of points that you've netted or grossed.

And so remember, when you add up your score,
In golf, much like life, as they say, "less is more."

Know the basic rule before you've begun:
However far it goes, each hit counts as one.

Both good shots and bad, long or short in this game,
Though it may seem unfair, they all count the same.

If you swing and you miss, and nowhere's where it went,
It counts, for like crime, it depends on intent.

There are shots you can hit, there are things you can do,
For which you're charged extra — not one stroke but two.

When the ball has been hit, where it's stopped and laid,
Unmoved and untouched is how it must be played.

You'll be penalized if the ball is moved,
And if even slightly, your lie is improved.

If your ball's in a "hazard," there's a prohibition
Against testing the ground or the hazard's condition.

(A "hazard"'s intended to get you confounded.
It's sand, turf or water where your club can't be grounded.)

▼▼▼

You can lift your ball, though, before you have hit,
To check to make sure that it isn't "unfit."

And lifting and cleaning the rules will condone,
When the ball is imbedded in a place "closely mown."

If you're told to speed up and you don't obey,
You'll be charged two strokes for "undue delay."

If a shot looks tricky and you ask for advice,
If it's not your partner, then two strokes is the price.

The rules have a section, albeit it's brief,
On when you're entitled to get some "relief."

You can move sticks and leaves —impediments "loose"—
But in a hazard, that will cost you a deuce.

If they're fixing the course, some lies won't be fair,
You don't have to hit from ground "under repair."

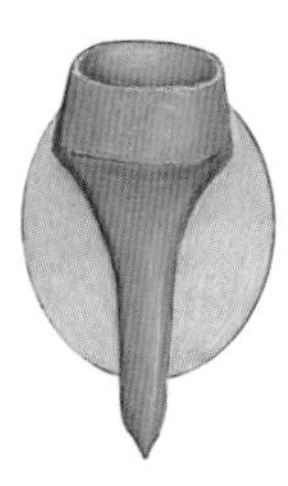

▼▼▼

The rules are quite different once the ball's on the green.
There, for example, you can lift and clean.

But some penalty strokes you're going to be spending,
If your putt hits the pin or the one who's tending.

The rules, though, don't tell you all you need to know
About all the places a golf ball can go.

A dog swallows your ball. How many strokes does that cost?
Is it unplayable, or treated as lost?

Say it lands in a branch — you can place it, but where?
Two club lengths away is still up in the air.

Or you'd rather not play it, for the ball's come to rest
Right in the middle of a live hornet's nest.

ETIQUETTE

▼▼▼

It's not enough, though, if the rules have been met.
You must also comply with the game's etiquette.

If you win, be modest. Golfers never gloat.
And during someone's swing you mustn't clear your throat.

Jingling change in your pants is quite poorly thought of,
As is ripping apart the velcro on your glove.

If your opponent's O.B., don't show that you're glad.
Hide your excitement. Look concerned. Say: "Too bad."

If you are winning, your manners are poor
To remind the one losing stroke by stroke of his score.

It's OK, though, to win by getting him outwitted.
Try playing with his mind. Gamesmanship's permitted.

If his putts are dropping, it's okay to instill doubt
By asking: "When you putt, do you breathe in or out?"

Many a player was doing fine but blew it
When asked: "You're swinging well. Just how do you do it?"

Or if his swing is steady, and you're afraid you'll lose.
You might get him thinking. Ask: "Which muscles do you use?"

Use gamesmanship sparely, for if it becomes known
That you do this often, you'll be playing alone.

THE COURSE

▼ ▼ ▼

The game of golf's not played on a field or a court.
You need vast expanses of land for this sport.

A golf course has segments, each with tee and a green.
Short ones have nine, but most are eighteen.

Because a little cup on the green is the goal,
Each of these segments is known as a "hole."

Holes vary in length from the cup to the tee.
They come in three sizes, pars five, four and three.

(A par is the score a good player should get.
With less he's quite pleased, with more he's upset.)

Regardless of length, each hole has a mission:
To make you count your score using long addition.

Oh sure there's the fairway, where they carefully mow.
On either side, though, they let the grass grow.

All but long and straight drives will end up in this "rough,"
Where the ball can hide and get lost in this stuff.

Beyond the deep rough there are trees and bushes
To ensnare bad shots — severe pulls or pushes.

▼ ▼ ▼

In less rural courses, a slice or duck hook
Could crash through a window into a breakfast nook.

At seaside courses, the wrong swing motion
Can send the ball to the beach, the rocks or the ocean.

Out of bounds in deserts aren't leafy or floral.
You'll find cacti and snakes, both rattler and coral.

Some holes have humps, like the back of a hog.
While others are crooked, like the leg of a dog.

In front of the green, to prevent ease of entry,
A bunker may stand, like a guard or sentry.

Sooner or later, you'll get on the green
Where the surface, though smooth, can be brutally mean.

Some courses make their greens as fast as they're able.
It's like trying to putt on the top of a table.

Most walk off the course, with egos deflated
Never having the score they anticipated.

The course lets you think, though, that you're on the right track.
It allows one good shot, and you keep coming back.

And so we forget each time we begin
That, like the house in gambling, the course always will win.

THE MATCH

▼▼▼

You've watched countless tapes, read books and had lessons.
You've even had some sports psychology sessions.

You bought woods and irons and the rest of the gear.
That car your wife wanted? It will wait 'til next year.

It's time now, you think, to get into the loop:
At the cooler you ask: "Can I join this group?"

You talk Ryder Cup points and know what that means.
(By now you're subscribing to three golf magazines.)

The boss ("B.J.") shows up, and you lay on some more.
He says: "Join us on Sunday. You'll be number four."

That Saturday night is one without rest.
You know the next day's round will be tough — and a test.

You find your way to the course, and whistling a song,
You stroll to the first tee as though you belong.

B.J. says: "Our game isn't for wusses or weenies.
We play all of the trash, like 'barkies' and 'greenies'."

"A ten dollar Nassau, and so no one has to guess.
When someone's two down, we automatically press."

THE FRONT NINE

▼ ▼ ▼

"Number one," says B.J. " is a little bit tight.
There's a cliff on the left, deep woods on the right."

What your drive must carry makes your knees quiver.
They call it a stream, but it looks like a river.

You look down the fairway; it's the longest you've seen.
"One question," you say: "Does this hole have a green?"

B.J. drives first, still chomping his cigar.
You never would have thought a ball could go that far.

As your turn approaches, you're suddenly concerned.
You realize you forgot everything that you learned.

You swing several times, but the ball hasn't moved.
Then someone whispers: "At least his swing's grooved."

You try to relax, but you can't, you're scared stiff.
B.J. says: "Nice work. You've mastered the whiff."

You concentrate hard, "Head down. Big pivot."
Though the golf ball stays put, you get nice length from your divot.

When you finally connect, it's less a hit than a nick.
The guy you're paired with looks as though he'll be sick.

▼▼▼

Your ball grazes the boss. He grunts: "This guy's a menace,"
Then adds: "Here's a thought... have you considered tennis?"

You're a total wreck now. Your mind has gone blank.
You hear: "He's improving. He's progressed to the shank."

Several shots later (the green's not yet in view),
You've already shot par, by a factor of two.

"You may not," says your partner, "have heard this before.
But in golf we don't try to run up the score."

On the first hole you lose two points and some trash.
You begin to wonder if you've brought enough cash.

Your partner's displeasure he doesn't try to hide.
As you walk off the green, he pulls you aside.

"If you say that you've hurt your wrist or your hand,
And want to go home, we'll all understand."

On hole number three, adding more to the pain,
The skies open up, and it starts to rain.

Though you start to loosen as the round progresses,
At the turn you're down one side and three presses.

▼▼▼

You realize all you've heard from your partner all day
Is "Time to pick up," or "You're still away."

You know your partner wants to get you ditched
When you hear him ask: "Should teams now be switched?"

But he stops all talk of partner swapping
When you start hitting them straight, and your putts start dropping.

The rain has stopped, and just like the weather,
Your game has improved and starts coming together.

On the 12th tee the boss starts getting annoyed.
His drive, a huge slice, sails O.B. to the void.

He retees, but this time his ball finds a trap.
You watch him bend his club until you see it snap.

B.J.'s smile is gone, and he's started to brood.
"Great," your partner whispers. "He's completely unglued."

You win that hole, the next, and you keep on winning.
Your partner, now your buddy, he can't stop grinning.

B.J., by contrast, is tearing his hair.
As you walk up eighteen, you've caught up. It's all square.

▼ ▼ ▼

The match and your day in the great outdoors
Come down to the last hole, the last putt—and it's yours.

It's outside the leather by barely an inch.
Though not quite a gimmie, it should be a cinch.

Sink it or miss it? Which one do you choose?
B.J. gives you a glare. The man hates to lose.

As he walks slowly by, you hear him mutter:
"Now don't be foolish when you swing that putter."

Your partner says: "Buddy, this is no time to choke.
Just keep your head steady, give it a firm stroke."

You swing at the ball, which by now is a blur.
Did you try to make it? You realize you're not sure.

"Nice try," B.J. says. "Jerk," you hear your partner snort.
The putt, a two footer, stops at least one foot short.

Feeling quite sheepish, you replace the flag,
As your partner (teeth clenched) looks into B.J.'s bag.

▼▼▼

Counting the clubs, he says: "Wait just one minute.
You've got fifteen, B.J. — one over the limit."

"I'm so sorry," he adds. "I hate to win this way.
But you broke Rule 4-4, subparagraph A."

B.J.'s ear to ear grin quickly turns to a frown.
He thought he'd won, one up, but he's lost — two down.

He stares hard at you, as he, the loser pays.
"It'll be some time," he says "before you need a raise."

Now that you have won, you've got a new fear;
Beating the boss at golf — will this hurt your career?

As you limp to your car, you give thought to this game,
And you realize just how the sport got its name.

It's a four letter word, but it isn't a curse.
They took the word "flog" and spelled it in reverse.

But if your job, one day, becomes less than secure
You might pack it all in and try out for the Tour.

Although time's going by, you gain years but not strength,
You saw Woods miss from five feet; you once made one that length.

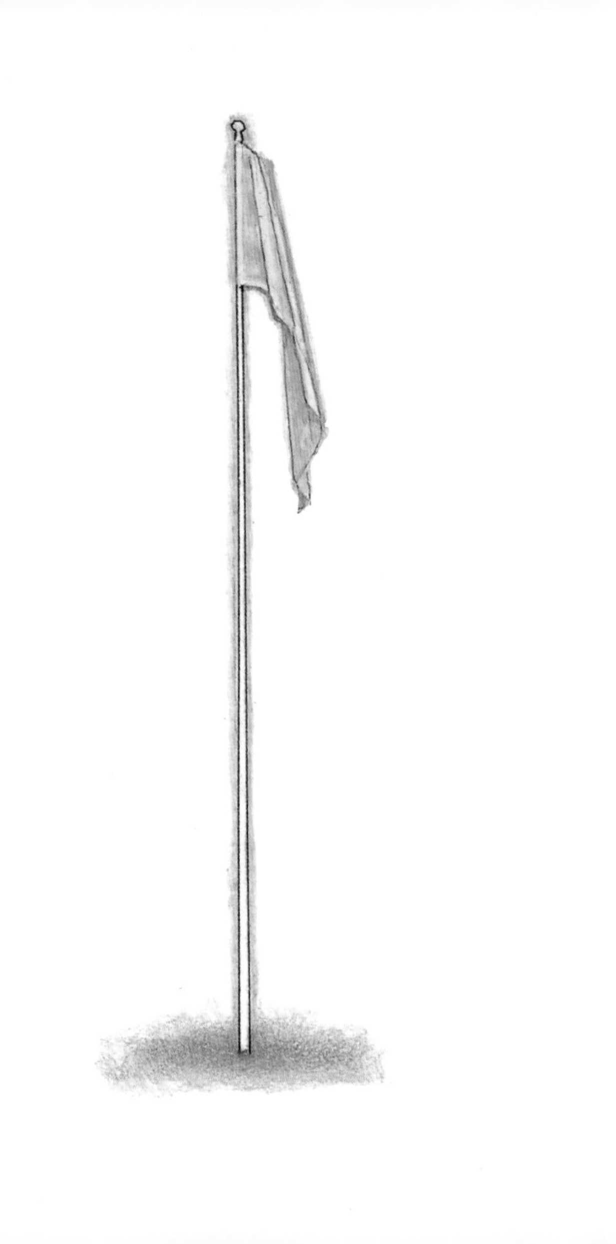